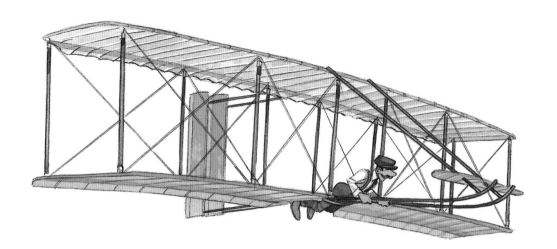

Author:
Ian Graham studied applied physics at City University in London. He then received a graduate degree in journalism, specializing in science and technology. Since becoming a freelance author and journalist, he has written more than one hundred children's nonfiction books.

Artist:
David Antram was born in Brighton, England, in 1958. He studied at Eastbourne College of Art and then worked in advertising for 15 years before becoming a full-time artist. He has illustrated many children's nonfiction books.

Series creator:
David Salariya was born in Dundee, Scotland. He has illustrated a wide range of books and has created and designed many new series for publishers in the UK and overseas. David established The Salariya Book Company in 1989. He lives in Brighton with his wife, illustrator Shirley Willis, and their son, Jonathan.

Editor: **Stephen Haynes**

Editorial Assistant: **Mark Williams**

PAPER FROM
SUSTAINABLE
FORESTS

© The Salariya Book Company Ltd MMXIII
No part of this publication may be reproduced in whole or in part, or stored in a retrieval system, or transmitted in any form or by any means, electronic, mechanical, photocopying, recording, or otherwise, without written permission of the publisher. For information regarding permission, write to the copyright holder.

Published in Great Britain in 2013 by
The Salariya Book Company Ltd
25 Marlborough Place, Brighton BN1 1UB

ISBN-13: 978-0-531-25945-0 (lib. bdg.)   978-0-531-23042-8 (pbk.)

All rights reserved.
Published in 2013 in the United States
by Franklin Watts
An imprint of Scholastic Inc.
Published simultaneously in Canada.

A CIP catalog record for this book is available
from the Library of Congress.

Printed and bound in China.
Printed on paper from sustainable sources.
1 2 3 4 5 6 7 8 9 10 R 22 21 20 19 18 17 16 15 14 13

SCHOLASTIC, FRANKLIN WATTS, and associated logos are trademarks and/or registered trademarks of Scholastic Inc.

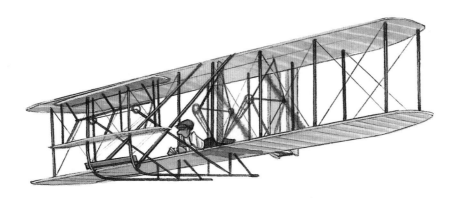

You Wouldn't Want to Be on the
First Flying Machine!

Written by
Ian Graham

Illustrated by
David Antram

Created and designed by
David Salariya

A High-Soaring Ride You'd Rather Not Take

Franklin Watts®
An Imprint of Scholastic Inc.
NEW YORK • TORONTO • LONDON • AUCKLAND • SYDNEY
MEXICO CITY • NEW DELHI • HONG KONG
DANBURY, CONNECTICUT

Contents

Introduction

It is the late 1800s. Birds fly; people don't. That's how it's been for as long as anyone can remember. It is the way the world is meant to be, or so most people think. But there are a few who think it really might be possible to build machines that actually fly. Some people think those people are crazy. Others think that people are not meant to fly and it is dangerous to go against the "natural order."

Orville

Wilbur

You are Orville Wright. You and your older brother, Wilbur, first get involved with flying machines in the 1890s. By this time, there have been hundreds of years of attempts to build heavier-than-air flying machines. They have all failed.

At first, would-be aviators tried to copy nature. They hurled themselves off towers and hills wearing birdlike wings. Instead of gliding down gracefully, most of them crashed to the ground in a tangled heap. For some, it was the last thing they ever did. It would seem that humans are indeed not meant to fly.

YOU WERE BORN on August 19, 1871, in Dayton, Ohio. Your brother Wilbur was born on April 16, 1867, near Millville, Indiana.

Wilbur, sad to say, will become sick and die in 1912, at the age of 45. You will live until 1948, witnessing the age of the jet plane.

Eventually, a handful of inventors finally begin to understand the science of flight. They try different shapes and sizes of wings and learn which is best. They build gliders that sail on the wind. Then you and your brother Wilbur decide to try your hand at building flying machines. You will change the course of history!

5

Inspirations

In 1878, when you are seven years old and Wilbur is 11, your father brings home a toy helicopter. Flying toys have been made for at least 500 years. You both enjoy flying your toy and even make your own copies of it.

When you grow up, you work in the family's bicycle shop in Dayton, Ohio. In the 1890s, newspaper stories about gliders big enough to carry a person inspire you to study flight again. You read everything you can find about flying machines and decide to try building your own. When you begin, you think they probably won't be successful.

Toy helicopter like the one given to the Wright brothers

Flap Flap

Why Can't We Fly?

Wings and feathers

Strong chest muscles

Weak chest muscles

Heavy build

COMPARED TO BIRDS, we are very heavy and our bodies aren't streamlined. We also don't have wings!

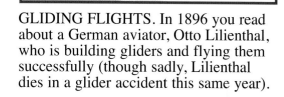

GLIDING FLIGHTS. In 1896 you read about a German aviator, Otto Lilienthal, who is building gliders and flying them successfully (though sadly, Lilienthal dies in a glider accident this same year).

6

Whoosh!

Creak

They make it look so easy...

CONTROL. Pilots control their gliders by shifting their body weight. You think there must be a better way to steer.

YOU AND WILBUR have built model aircraft since childhood. Your father encourages you to solve problems by looking for the answers in books.

FLAPPERS. Some people try to build full-size copies of ornithopters—flying toys with flapping wings (left). None of them work.

7

On a Wing and a Prayer

You and your brother want to build a powered airplane, but you decide to build a glider before you tackle something with an engine. That means designing wings. But what shape should they be? And how big? You make small models to try out different shapes. Then in 1899 you build a much bigger model with a wingspan of 5 feet (1.5 meters). You choose a biplane design—with two wings, one above the other. It isn't big enough to carry a person, but you can fly it as a kite.

Hold onto me, Wilbur!

The biplane is made from a wooden frame covered with fabric. You paint it with a type of varnish to seal the fabric so that air can't blow through it. When you try it, it actually flies! In a strong gust of wind, it can lift you off the ground. Your next step is to build a glider big enough to carry a man!

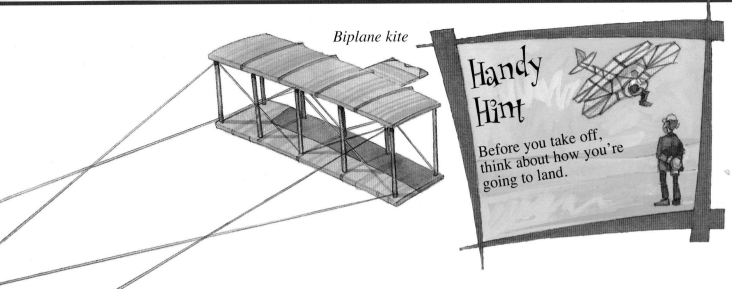

Biplane kite

Handy Hint

Before you take off, think about how you're going to land.

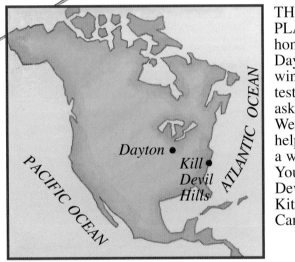

THE PERFECT PLACE. Your hometown of Dayton, Ohio, isn't windy enough to test gliders. You ask the U.S. Weather Bureau to help you find a windier place. You choose Kill Devil Hills, near Kitty Hawk, North Carolina.

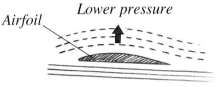

Lower pressure

Airfoil

THE CURVED SHAPE of a wing, called an *airfoil*, creates an upward force, called *lift*. The curved top makes the air flowing over it speed up. According to Bernoulli's Principle, speeding up air lowers its pressure. Lowering air pressure above a wing causes the air below to move upward, lifting the wing.

Do you think it's windy enough here, Orville?

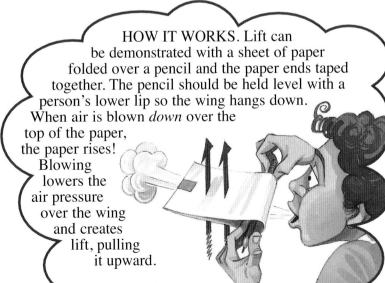

HOW IT WORKS. Lift can be demonstrated with a sheet of paper folded over a pencil and the paper ends taped together. The pencil should be held level with a person's lower lip so the wing hangs down. When air is blown *down* over the top of the paper, the paper rises! Blowing lowers the air pressure over the wing and creates lift, pulling it upward.

The First Gliders

Your first full-size glider has a wingspan of 17 feet (5.2 m). The pilot lies on the lower wing. He climbs or dives by tilting an "elevator" at the front. The challenge is to balance the glider. If you don't balance a bicycle, it will crash, and the same is true of an aircraft. You and Wilbur develop a balancing system of pulling wires to twist the glider's wingtips. You call it "wing warping." Sadly, your glider doesn't fly very well and the next one you build is even worse! Your designs rely on research done by Otto Lilienthal. Perhaps he got it wrong?

Stopwatch

STOPWATCH.
All of the glider flights are timed to the precise second.

A CLINOMETER is used to measure how steeply each glider climbs or dives.

Clinometer

Wheeze!

ANEMOMETER.
Wind speed is measured with an anemometer. Its propeller spins and a dial shows the speed.

Tape measure

PLAGUED BY MOSQUITOES. Living at Kill Devil Hills is no picnic! Mosquitoes swarm over the dunes. You write home: "They chew us clear through our underwear and socks. Lumps begin swelling up all over my body like hen's eggs!"

TAPE MEASURE.
You measure the lengths of all your flights with a tape measure.

Anemometer

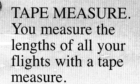

Throb

You should get more exercise, Wilbur.

Handy Hint

Don't let the plane's nose tip up too much. This disturbs the airflow over the wings, and the plane will stall.

Elevator

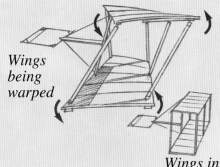

Wings being warped

Wings in normal position

WING WARPING makes a plane roll to one side by changing the shape of its wings. The wingtips on one side twist up at the front and down at the back, producing more lift. The other wingtips twist in the opposite direction, producing less lift.

AN AIRCRAFT can move in three different ways: pitch, roll, and yaw.

PITCH. An aircraft's pitch changes when its nose rises or falls.

ROLL. An aircraft rolls, or banks, when one wing rises and the other falls.

YAW. An aircraft yaws when its nose turns to the left or right.

Back to the Drawing Board

You now realize that you are not going to make further progress by relying on facts and figures from other people, so you decide to do your own research. In 1901 you go home to Dayton with notes on the flights you have made that year. You build all sorts of devices to test different shapes of wings. Since you don't have much money, everything is built using the materials, tools, and equipment you already have on hand. This includes a test machine made from a bicycle; and a wind tunnel made from a wooden box, a fan, and your workshop motor. Armed with your own research results, you can now start work on designing a completely new glider.

BICYCLE TEST RIG. The bicycle has an extra wheel on top with a flat plate on one side and a model wing (airfoil), standing on end, on the other side. As you ride, wind hits the plate and the wing tries to turn the wheel in opposite directions. By trying different model wings and seeing how much the wheel turns, you can tell which wing is best.

Model wing

Flat plate

12 *Bicycle test rig*

Wind tunnel

WIND TUNNEL. The most useful of all your test machines is a wind tunnel. A fan blows air through it at approximately 30 miles (48 kilometers) per hour so that you can test different-shaped wings.

Handy Hint

Wind tunnels will become an essential tool for testing aircraft designs.

I prefer the kind of plane that stays on the ground.

Your workshop

Perfection!

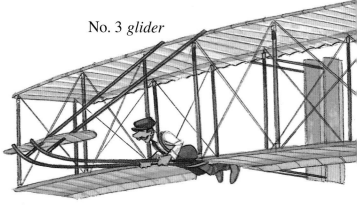

No. 3 *glider*

In 1902, after experimenting with different glider designs, you and Wilbur go back to Kitty Hawk with a new glider, *No. 3*. This has been designed using the results of your latest research and tests. Its wings are longer and narrower than earlier gliders and it has two tall vanes at the back. It works better than your previous designs, but there are still a few problems to iron out. You find it flies better with the wingtips bent slightly downward, and the tail needs some changes to make it easier to control in turns. By the time you've finished with it, *No. 3* is the world's first fully controllable aircraft. It is so successful that you decide you are ready to move on to the next step—building a powered aircraft.

THE *No. 3* WRIGHT GLIDER of 1902 looks slender and graceful because of its longer, narrower wings (above). After all the research that went into its design, it flies beautifully too.

However, *No. 3* can be tricky in turns. One time when you are piloting it, it slides sideways and slams into the ground. Luckily, you are dazed but uninjured.

I think we need to look at the tail.

RUDDER. You decide to change the tail so that it has one movable vane—a rudder (below)—instead of two fixed vanes. This gives the pilot more control in turns.

TURNING PROBLEM. You discuss how to solve the problem of sliding in turns by changing the glider's tail.

Rudder swivels when wings warp

Wing-warping cradle (operated by pilot's hips)

THE TAIL is finally linked to the wing-warping cradle (below). Now, when the glider rolls, the tail swivels automatically and keeps the aircraft under control. Perfection!

Elevator control

Bonk!

15

Power

It is calculated that you need an 8-horsepower engine weighing up to 181 pounds (82 kilograms) to power your new aircraft. At first you think you'll be able to buy one from one of the many engine-making companies you know. But when the time comes, you can't get what you want—so you and your brother decide to build the engine yourselves! Your bicycle mechanic, Charles Taylor, helps with the design and then builds it for you. It has four cylinders and burns ordinary gasoline. It is ready for testing in only six weeks. Your engine is good enough for the short test flights you are planning—if your aircraft takes off!

BUILD IT YOURSELF. Your mechanic, Charles Taylor, builds your engine without any detailed plans (above). You and Wilbur sketch the parts you need and Taylor makes them. Amazingly, it actually works!

WANTED: ONE ENGINE. You and Wilbur write to suppliers with details of the engine you need. But none are able to supply the right engine at the right price.

Handy Hint

If you want a job done properly, do it yourself.

SUCCESS! The finished engine is lighter and more powerful than you expected. This means you can make the plane heavier and stronger and it will still take off—you hope!

Engine made by Charles Taylor and the Wright brothers

Spinning Props

An engine cannot fly an airplane by itself. A propeller is needed to push an aircraft through the air. You and Wilbur think you can simply redesign ship propellers to produce a propeller that works in air. But you are amazed to find that ship propellers are made by trial and error! You first have to figure out how ship propellers function before designing your own propellers. You decide to use two, driven by chains from the engine. Mounting the propellers behind the wings means that they won't interfere with the smooth airflow over the wings.

So why are they this shape, Orville?

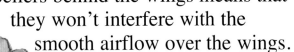

You have a terrible temper!

I have a terrible temper?

ARGUMENTS. You and your brother are great arguers. You often hash out tricky problems by shouting at each other at the top of your lungs!

SHIP PROPELLERS. You and Wilbur want to model your airplane propellers on ship propellers. The trouble is, no one has properly figured out how to design them. Even the people who make ship propellers don't know why they are the shape they are!

They don't seem to know, Wilbur!

Handy Hint

Make your two propellers turn in opposite directions. Then the plane won't pull to one side as it flies.

THE WRIGHT PROPELLERS are tested to make sure your theories and calculations are correct. Each wooden propeller is 8.5 feet (2.6 m) from tip to tip.

Whirr

Building the Flyer

Your first powered aircraft, the *Flyer*, has a wooden frame and a wingspan of 40 feet (12.2 m). There are two elevators at the front and two rudders at the back. The wings, elevators, and rudders are covered with fabric. The engine is mounted on the lower wing.

But there is still no seat! The pilot lies on his stomach in a cradle that slides from side to side to warp the wings. There are no wheels either. The *Flyer* rests on a trolley on a long rail. When the plane takes off, the trolley falls away. When it lands again, it simply skids to a halt on the ground.

Elevators

MAKING A WING. *Flyer*'s wings are made from wooden ribs running from front to back. These are attached to beams called spars, which run the length of the wings. Cloth is then stretched over the top and bottom surfaces of each wing.

Wooden ribs

Fabric covering

Wooden spar

Handy Hint

Wood is the perfect material for ribs and spars because it is light, strong, and flexible.

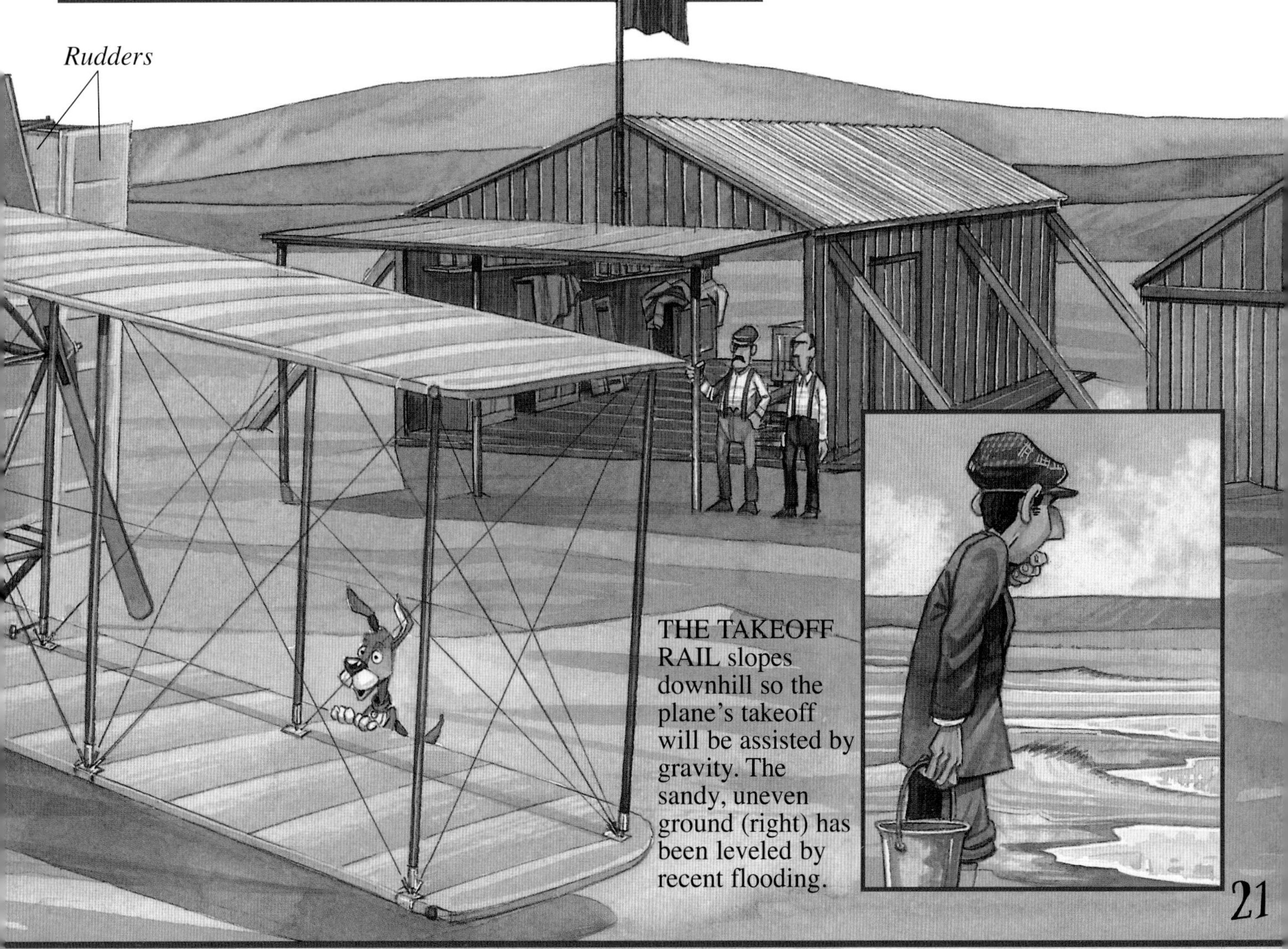

Rudders

THE TAKEOFF RAIL slopes downhill so the plane's takeoff will be assisted by gravity. The sandy, uneven ground (right) has been leveled by recent flooding.

The First Flight...Ever!

Preparations for the first flight are made on the morning of December 14, 1903. You toss a coin to decide who will pilot the *Flyer*. Wilbur wins. He lies down in the warp cradle and the engine is started. The plane moves away down the launch rail, gathers speed, and lifts off.

Then, disaster! It plows into the sand!

It is December 17 before you can try again. Now it's your turn to be pilot. Five other people witness this attempt. This time, the plane sails away into the wind and lands 12 seconds later, approximately 120 feet (36 m) away. You make three more flights that day. You have made history!

BE PATIENT. Wind conditions have to be just right before you can attempt a takeoff.

I've never used a camera before!

START THE ENGINE. The plane is held while the engine starts. When it reaches full speed, the plane is released.

GET READY. You lend your camera to one of the witnesses, John Daniels, who aims it at the spot where the *Flyer* is expected to leave the ground.

Image of the first flight, December 17, 1903

Handy Hint

Raise a red flag to summon the lifeguards from the nearby beach. They'll help you move the plane, and act as witnesses too.

DANIELS PRESSES THE BUTTON at the right moment to take a historic photograph (similar to the image above) of the first airplane flight!

They done it!
They done it!

23

And Now, Next Year's Model

Making history once would be enough for most people, but not Wilbur and Orville Wright! Now you build a series of new planes, each improving on the one before. The first is *Flyer II*, built in 1904. Greater engine power means that you don't need strong winds to take off, so you leave Kitty Hawk and start flying at Huffman Prairie, closer to your home in Dayton. In 1905 you build *Flyer III*. This is the first really practical airplane, and you finally have an aircraft that can make longer flights. You can bank, turn, fly in circles, make figure eights, whatever you want. *Flyer III*'s longest flight lasts for 39 minutes.

FLYER II. At Huffman Prairie you practice with *Flyer II* to learn how to control a plane in the air.

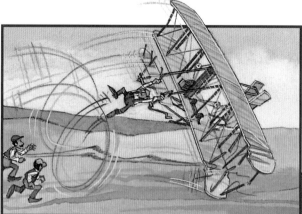

THE END OF THE ORIGINAL *FLYER*. Later in the same day as its first historic flights, the original *Flyer* was hit by a gust of wind. John Daniels tried to hold it down, but it turned over, injuring him. *Flyer* was damaged so badly that it never flew again.

Spot the Difference

Flyer I, *1903*

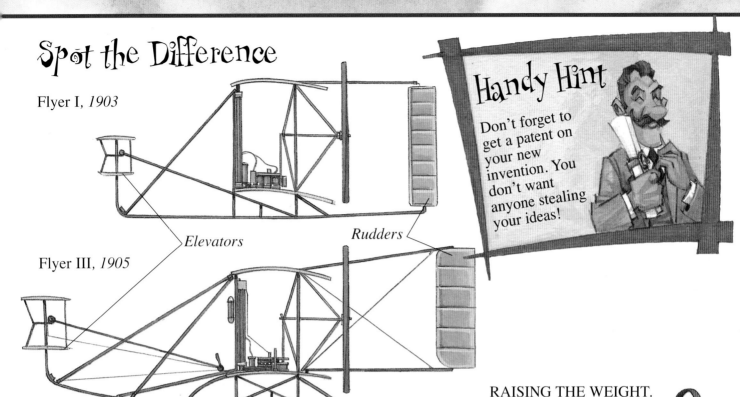

Elevators

Rudders

Handy Hint

Don't forget to get a patent on your new invention. You don't want anyone stealing your ideas!

Flyer III, *1905*

FLYER III is longer than the earlier models. Its elevators are farther forward and its rudders are farther back. This makes it easier to control.

RAISING THE WEIGHT. Before each flight, the 1,600-pound (726 kg) weight has to be raised to the top of the tower (right). It is usually done by a group of volunteers pulling on a rope. Then the rope is hooked up to the plane.

Weight

Pulleys

LAUNCHING ALONG A RAIL. The wind isn't always right for takeoff, so you invent a way to take off that doesn't rely on the wind. A falling weight tugs a rope that pulls the airplane along its launch rail.

Launch system with weight, pulleys, and rail

Rail

Look! He's flying!

Take a Seat

In 1907 you and Wilbur finally build an airplane with a seat! The *Type A*, as it becomes known, is an improved version of *Flyer III*. Not only does it have a seat for the pilot, but also one for a passenger. The first airplane passengers experience the magic of flight in 1908. They sit on the wing with the pilot, so it is a very windy experience. That can cause problems, because of the fashions of the day. Any woman who flies as a passenger has to have her long skirt tied up with string to preserve her modesty! Now that the pilot is sitting up and not lying in a warp cradle, he can't slide to each side to warp the wings and bank (roll) the plane. Instead, he uses control sticks to move the rudders, wings, and elevators.

Flight Controls

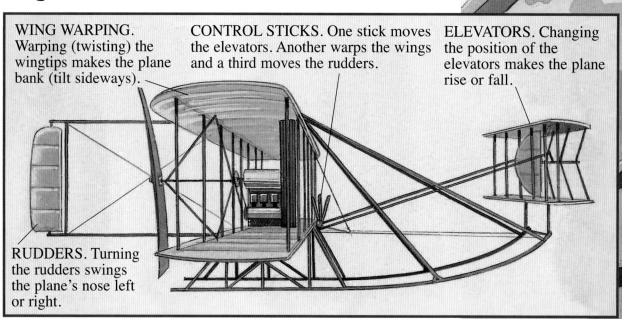

WING WARPING. Warping (twisting) the wingtips makes the plane bank (tilt sideways).

CONTROL STICKS. One stick moves the elevators. Another warps the wings and a third moves the rudders.

ELEVATORS. Changing the position of the elevators makes the plane rise or fall.

RUDDERS. Turning the rudders swings the plane's nose left or right.

Showing the World

In 1908 Wilbur makes flights in France, while you demonstrate the plane to the U.S. Army. (The army was offered a Wright plane in 1905, but thought the idea of military airplanes was ridiculous!)

All goes well until you take Lieutenant T. E. Selfridge up for a flight. Disaster strikes—you crash and Selfridge is killed. The army buys the plane anyway.

Meanwhile, when the French see Wilbur flying so gracefully, they are amazed. Count de La Vaulx says the Wright plane has "revolutionized the aviator's world."

WILBUR'S FLIGHTS IN FRANCE are front-page news everywhere. This magazine cover (above) shows him flying at Hunaudières Racecourse, near Le Mans, in 1908.

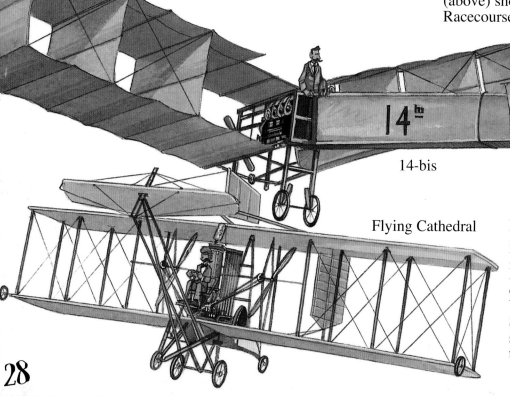

14-bis

Flying Cathedral

EUROPEAN AVIATORS are years behind you. In France, Alberto Santos-Dumont builds an odd airplane called *14-bis*. In Britain, the Wild West showman Colonel S. F. Cody is flying an airplane so huge that it is nicknamed the *Flying Cathedral*!

Air Crash Investigation

YOUR CRASH with Lt. Selfridge is caused by a cracked propeller that starts vibrating (1).

The shaking loosens the propeller shaft and one of the propeller blades cuts through a rudder cable (2).

The loose ends of the wire wind around the propeller blade (3) and tear it off completely (4).

You stop the engine and try to land, but the plane nose-dives into the ground.

Handy Hint

Don't be discouraged by this disaster. One day, planes will be one of the safest ways to travel.

I'll be advising the army not to buy this thing!

29

Glossary

Aileron Part of an aircraft's wing that swivels up or down to make the plane roll or bank.

Airfoil The special curved shape of a wing, designed to produce lift.

Anemometer An instrument for measuring wind speed.

Aviator An early word for a pilot.

Bank To roll an aircraft over to one side to make a turn.

Biplane An airplane with two wings, one above the other.

Clinometer An instrument for measuring how steep a slope is.

Cylinder The tube-shaped part inside a gasoline engine where the gas is burned.

Elevator The part of an aircraft that tilts to make the plane climb or dive.

Glider An aircraft designed to fly without an engine.

Heavier-than-air flying machine Any kind of aircraft other than a balloon or airship. Balloons and airships are lighter than air because they are filled with hot air or lightweight gas.

Lift The upward force produced by a wing that makes an airplane rise into the air.

Ornithopter A toy airplane with flapping wings. No one has made a successful full-size ornithopter.

Patent A document that gives legal protection to an invention, making it against the law for anyone to copy it.

Pitch A movement of an aircraft that makes its nose rise or fall.

Rib Part of the framework inside a wing; it runs from the front of the wing to the back.

Roll A movement of an aircraft that makes one wing rise and the other fall.

Rudder The part of an airplane's tail that swivels from side to side to make the plane's nose turn left or right.

Shaft A spinning rod in an engine.

Spar Part of the framework of an airplane's wing; it runs the length of the wing.

Stall A sudden loss of lift caused by flying too slowly or raising an aircraft's nose too high.

Vane An aircraft part in the shape of a fin or flat panel.

Warp cradle The wooden frame that the pilot of a Wright plane lay in and slid to one side or the other to make the aircraft bank.

Wind tunnel A tube or chamber through which air is blown by a fan, to test wings and other aircraft parts.

Wing Part of an aircraft designed to produce lift when it cuts through air.

Wingspan The width of an airplane from wingtip to wingtip.

Wing warping Twisting a plane's wingtips to make it roll or bank.

Yaw A movement of an aircraft that makes its nose turn to the right or left.

Index